Rising Stars Assessment

Science Progress Tests

Year 1

Pauline Hannigan

Series Advisors: Cornwall Learning

Rising Stars

Cornwall Learning

Rising Stars UK Ltd, 7 Hatchers Mews, Bermondsey Street, London SE1 3GS

www.risingstars-uk.com

Published 2014
Reprinted 2014 (three times), 2015 (twice)

All facts are correct at time of going to press. All referenced websites were correct at the time this book went to press.

Author: Pauline Hannigan
Educational consultant: Ed Walsh, Cornwall Learning
Accessibility reviewer: Vivien Kilburn
Editorial: Denise Moulton, Lynette Woodward and Susan Gardner
Typist: Rosalyn Dale
Design: Ray Rich and Clive Sutherland
Illustrations: Oxford Designers and Illustrators
Photos: istockphoto.com
Cover design: Burville-Riley Partnership

Rising Stars is grateful to the following people and schools who contributed to the development of these materials.
Plumcroft Primary School, London; Rainford Brook Lodge Primary School, Merseyside; St Nicholas CE Primary School, Chislehurst; St Margaret's CE Primary School, Heywood, Rochdale; Tennyson Road Primary School, Luton

British Library Cataloguing in Publication Data.
A CIP record for this book is available from the British Library.
ISBN: 978 1 84680 960 6

Printed by Ashford Colour Press

FSC
www.fsc.org
MIX
Paper from responsible sources
FSC® C011748

Contents

Introduction

Why use Rising Stars Assessment Progress Tests?

The *Rising Stars Assessment Science Progress Tests* have been developed to support teachers assess the progress their pupils are making against the 2014 National Curriculum Programme of Study for science. The tests are designed to support effective classroom assessment across Years 1 to 6 and are easy to use and mark.

The tests are organised around the topics in the Programme of Study and have been:

- written by primary science assessment specialists
- reviewed by primary science curriculum and assessment experts.

How do the tests track progress?

The results data from the tests can be used to track progress. They show whether pupils are making the expected progress for their year, more than expected progress or less than expected progress. This data can then be used alongside other evidence to enable effective planning of future teaching and learning, for reporting to parents and as evidence for Ofsted inspections. If teachers are using the CD-ROM version of the tests, the results data can be keyed into the Progress Tracker (see page 7 for more information) which automatically shows the progress of individual pupils against the Programme of Study and the results for all pupils by question and test. Data can also be exported into the school's management information system (MIS).

About the Science Progress Tests

The tests are written to match the content requirements of the Programme of Study for the 2014 National Curriculum. The content areas are:

Content	Year 1	Year 2	Year 3	Year 4	Year 5	Year 6
Living things (and their habitats)		✓		✓	✓	✓
Plants	✓	✓	✓			
Animals, including humans	✓	✓	✓	✓	✓	✓
Evolution and inheritance						✓
Materials (uses, properties and changes)	✓	✓			✓	
Rocks			✓			
States of matter				✓		
Light			✓			✓
Sound				✓		
Seasonal changes/Earth and space	✓				✓	
Forces (and magnets)			✓		✓	
Electricity				✓		✓

In line with the Programme of Study, the skills of working scientifically are assessed through all the content areas rather than separately. For each content area there are four tests:

- Test 1(diagnostic) – note that for Years 1 and 2 this is a checklist rather than a test to make it more accessible and informative for pupils whose written language skills are likely to be less developed

- Test 2(mid-topic)
- Test 3(end of topic)
- Test 4(end of year)

The marks for each test are as follows:

Test	Number of marks					
	Year 1	Year 2	Year 3	Year 4	Year 5	Year 6
Test/checklist 1 (diagnostic)	N/A	N/A	10	10	10	10
Test 2 (mid-topic)	10	10	10	10	10	10
Test 3 (end of topic)	10	10	10	10	10	10
Test 4 (end of year)	10	10	10	10	10	10

Test demand

The first test for each topic is designed to help teachers assess the prior learning of individual pupils and the class before teaching begins. These tests/checklists are more open-ended than tests 2–4 to elicit as much information as possible to help teachers to refine their plans for teaching the topic.

Test 2 is designed to be used during a topic, test 3 at the end of a topic and test 4 at the end of the year. Test 4 could optionally be used as an alternative or additional test at the end of a topic. Tests 2–4 follow the same approach. In each test:

- 5 marks are allocated to knowledge and understanding
- 5 marks are allocated to application
- 4 marks additionally assess working scientifically.

Tests 2–4 also contain a mix of objective questions, and questions requiring written answers.

Tracking progress

The marks pupils score in the tests can be used to track how they are progressing against the expected outcomes for their year group in relation to the National Curriculum Programme of Study. The marks for tests 2–4 for each topic have been split into three progress zones:

- less than expected progress
- expected progress
- more than expected progress.

The zones for each year group are as follows:

		Zone mark range		
	Test	Less than expected progress	Expected progress	More than expected progress
Year 1	2–4	0–5	6–8	9–10
Year 2	2–4	0–5	6–8	9–10
Year 3	2–4	0–5	6–8	9–10
Year 4	2–4	0–5	6–8	9–10
Year 5	2–4	0–5	6–8	9–10
Year 6	2–4	0–5	6–8	9–10

Determining prior learning

The first test for each topic is provided to help teachers find out about prior learning.

For Years 1 and 2 these tests are in the form of diagnostic checklists to enable an oral investigation of prior learning as it is recognised that pupils have limited reading and writing vocabularies, particularly in Year 1. Each checklist comprises a set of questions to ask pupils and supporting visual prompts. There is also a Pupil responses form that can be used to record whether some, most or all pupils are able to answer each question.

For Years 3–6 there is a diagnostic test for each topic. These tests can be administered as described below and the marks analysed to identify the prior learning of individual pupils and the class as a whole.

How to use the Science Progress Tests

Preparation and timings

1 Make enough copies of the test(s) for each pupil to have their own copy.
2 Hand out the papers and ensure pupils are seated appropriately so that they can't see each other's papers.
3 Pupils will need pens or pencils, rulers and erasers. Encourage pupils to cross out answers rather than rub them out.
4 There are no time limits for the tests but normal practice is to allow a minute per mark for written tests. Help with reading may be given using the same rules as when providing a reader with the DfE KS2 tests.

Supporting pupils during the tests

Before the test explain to the pupils that the test is an opportunity to show what they know, understand and can do. They should try to answer all the questions but should not worry if there are some they can't do.

Many pupils will be able to work independently in the tests, with minimal support from the teacher or a teaching assistant. However, pupils should be encouraged to 'have a go' at a question, or to move on to a fresh question if they appear to be stuck, to ensure that no pupil becomes distressed.

It is important that pupils receive appropriate support, but are not unfairly advantaged or disadvantaged. Throughout the tests, therefore, the teacher may read, explain or sign to a pupil any parts of the test that include instructions, for example by demonstrating how to circle an answer.

With younger age groups you may also consider using the version of the test on the CD-ROM and projecting it onto a whiteboard to support a whole class or group to take the tests. You may choose to refer to the words on the whiteboard and read them aloud so that pupils can follow them on the screen and on their own test paper and then write their answers on their papers individually.

Marking the tests

Use the detailed mark scheme and your professional judgement to award marks. **Do not award half marks.**

It is useful to use peer marking of test questions from time to time. Pupils should exchange test sheets and mark them as you read out the question and answer. You will need to check that pupils are marking accurately. This approach also provides an opportunity to recap on any questions that pupils found difficult to answer.

Feeding back to pupils

Once the test has been marked, use a five-minute feedback session with the pupils to help them review their answers. Wherever possible pupils should be encouraged to make their own corrections as in this way they will become more aware of their own strengths and weaknesses. Agree with each pupil what they did well in the test and what the targets are for them to improve. A template 'My Progress' sheet is provided on page 8 for this purpose. Encourage pupils to colour the face which best shows how well they think they did in the test (there are three faces to choose from – one happy, one sad, and one neutral). They should then add the number of the question that they found most difficult. Finally, pupils should fill in the speech bubble to indicate what they need more help with. Some pupils will be able to do this themselves but some may find a word bank supplied by the teacher useful. The teacher or another adult may need to act as scribe for some pupils.

Using the Progress Tracker

The table on page 5 gives the mark ranges for the progress zones for each test which you can use to see how well each pupil is doing in each test and across each topic. If pupils are making the expected progress for their year they will be consistently scoring marks in the middle zone of marks in the tests.

The CD-ROM* version of *Science Progress Tests* includes an interactive Progress Tracker, which allows you to enter the marks for each question for each test by pupil. This then automatically shows you which zone the pupil is in and also the zone distribution for the class so that you can track the progress of individual pupils and the whole class.

The Progress Tracker also enables you to review the marks for each question so that you can identify areas where some or all pupils may need further support and areas where some or all pupils are ready to be stretched further. It also provides a separate summary of marks for each pupil for knowledge and understanding, application and working scientifically so that you can identify if pupils have strengths or weaknesses in a particular area.

If required, data from the tests can be exported into the school's management information system (MIS) so that it can be used alongside other data in whole school monitoring including the monitoring of specific groups of pupils, such as Pupil Premium.

Full details about the Progress Tracker are provided on the CD-ROM.

* If you have the book version only of *Science Progress Tests*, the Progress Tracker can be downloaded from bit.ly/progtracker

My progress

Name: ______________________ Class: ____________ Date: ________

Test: ____

★ How well did you do?

★ Which question did you find the hardest?

★ What do you need more help with?

Year 1

Plants Test 1 (diagnostic assessment)

Question	Answer	Extra information
1. Can you tell me the name of a plant that you seen growing?	Specific name of any common plant, including flowering plants and trees	
2. Can you name any of these flowers?	Daisy, rose, dandelion, daffodil (or other commonly available flowers)	*Use real flowers or show the photographs provided on page 10.*
3. Can you tell me the name of a plant that people sometimes eat?	Any fruit or vegetable	
4. Can you tell me the name of a tree.	Any tree	Accept pine or evergreen
5. What is different about these two plants?	Shape/number/colour of leaves Shape/colour of flower, height of plant	*Use real plants or show the photographs provided on page 11.* Accept any reasonable difference
6. Name this part of the plant.	Leaf, stem, flower, root	*Use a real plant or show the picture provided on page 12.* Point to the parts.
7. These leaves are different shapes. How can we sort them into two groups?	Any two groups showing differences in leaves	*Use real leaves or show the photographs provided on page 13, to show leaves that can be readily sorted into two groups.*

Plants Test 1 (diagnostic assessment): pupil responses form

Q	Some pupils	Most pupils	All pupils
1.			
2.			
3.			
4.			
5.			
6.			
7.			

Plants Test 1 (diagnostic assessment): question 2, visual prompts

Plants Test 1 (diagnostic assessment): question 5, visual prompts

Year 1

Plants Test 1 (diagnostic assessment): question 6, visual prompt

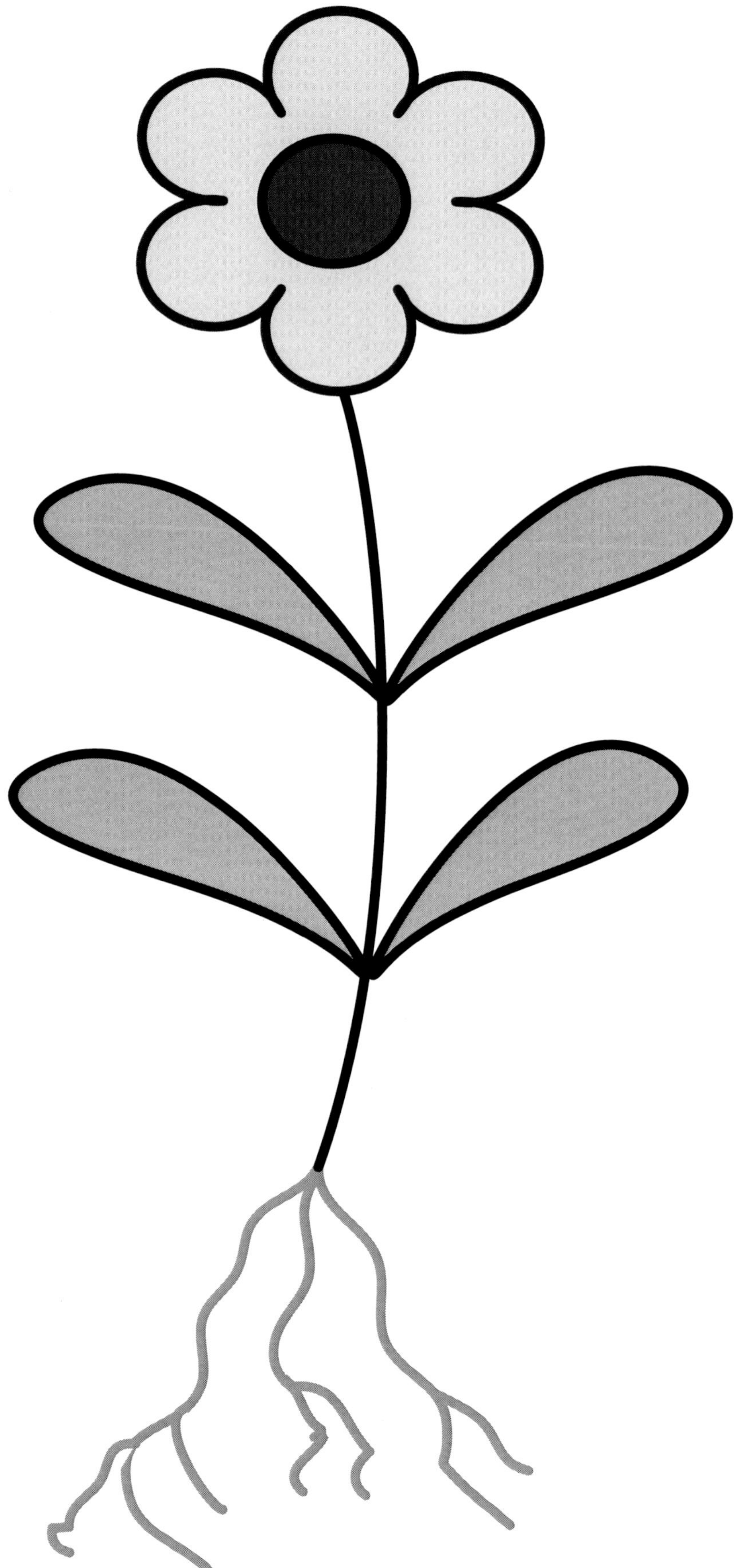

Plants Test 1 (diagnostic assessment): question 7, visual prompts

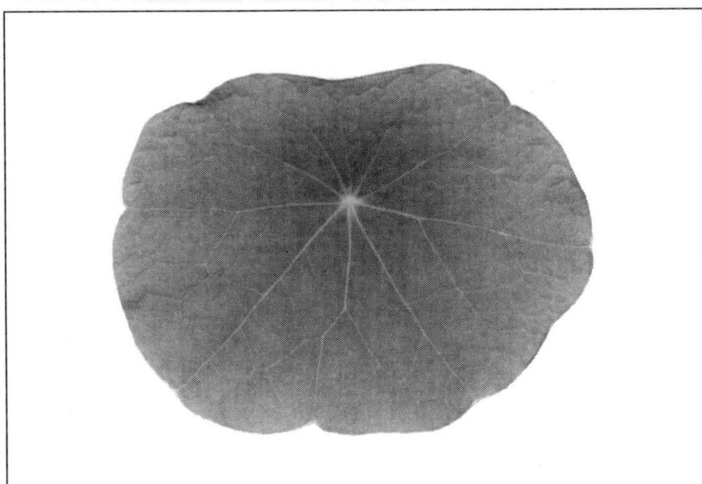

Year 1

Plants Test 2 (mid-topic)

Name: ______________________ Class: ____________ Date: __________

1. Join the labels to the plant.

roots	stem
flower	leaf

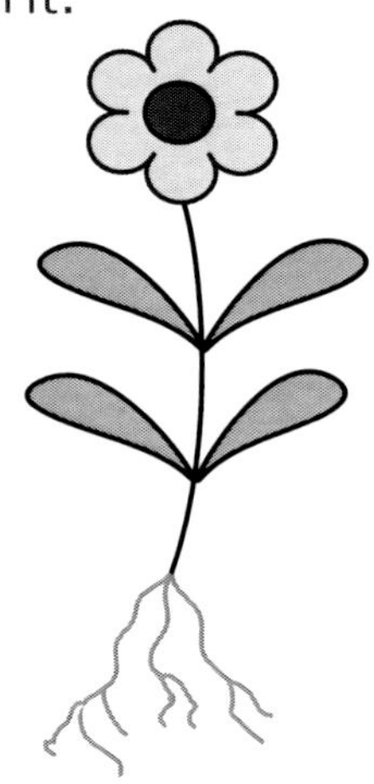

KU

2 marks

2. **a)** Write **two** things that are different about these flowers.

i) ....

ii) ....

KU

2 marks

b) What is this part of the flower called?

....

KU

1 mark

Total for this page

3. a) What can Tomas use to help him see the flowers in more detail?

Tick the correct answer.

A/WS ☐ 1 mark

b) How would you use it?

A ☐ 1 mark

4. a) Sort these leaves into **two** groups. Draw arrows.

A/WS ☐ 1 mark

b) How did you choose where to put them?

A/WS ☐ 1 mark

c) Draw **one** more leaf in **one** of the ovals.

A/WS ☐ 1 mark

/10 **Total for this test**

Year 1

Plants Test 3 (end of topic)

Name: ______________________ Class: ______________ Date: __________

1. **a)** Label the tree.

KU
2 marks

b) Here is the same tree.

The leaves have fallen off. Why?

....

KU
1 mark

c) What happens to the leaves before they fall off the tree?

....

....

KU
1 mark

Total for this page

2. Write down the name of a tree.

KU
1 mark

3. Plants grow.

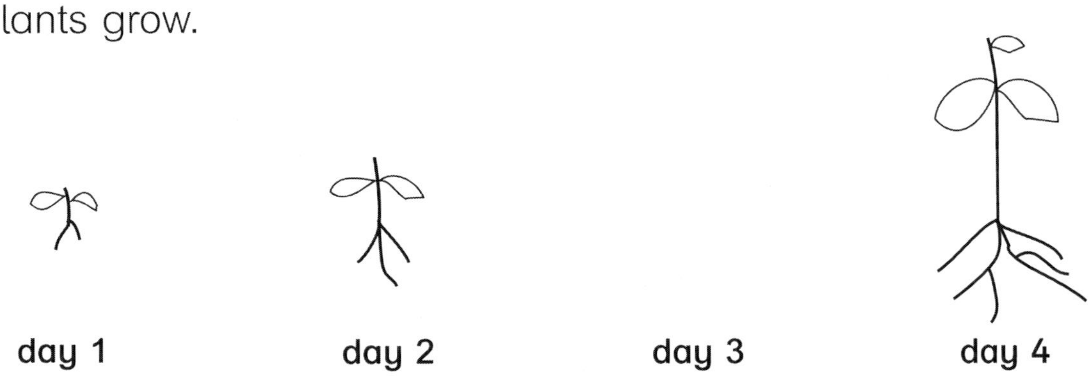

A/WS
2 marks

a) Look at the table. Draw the plant on day 3.

b) Fill in the gaps in this table.

Day	Number of leaves	Number of roots
1	2	2
2	2	
3	2	5
4		6

A/WS
2 marks

c) What has happened to the stem on day 3?

A
1 mark

/10
Total for this test

Year 1
Plants Test 4 (end of year)

Name: ______________________ Class: ______________ Date: __________

1. What will this tree look like in the winter?

....

....

KU

☐

1 mark

2. **a)** What sort of plants do all of these fruits and seeds come from?

....

KU

☐

1 mark

b) Write **two** differences between these seeds.

i) ....

ii) ....

A/WS

☐

2 marks

☐

Total for this page

3. Tick the plants that are food for us.

 ☐
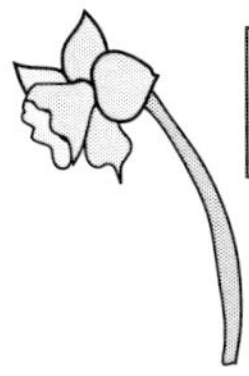 ☐
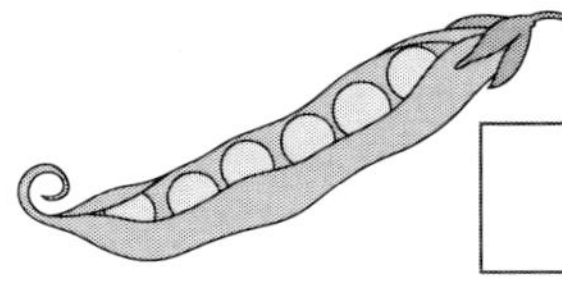 ☐
 ☐

KU
1 mark

4.

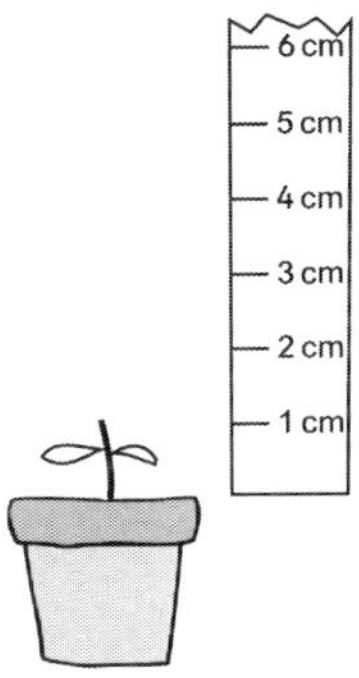

day 1: 1 cm

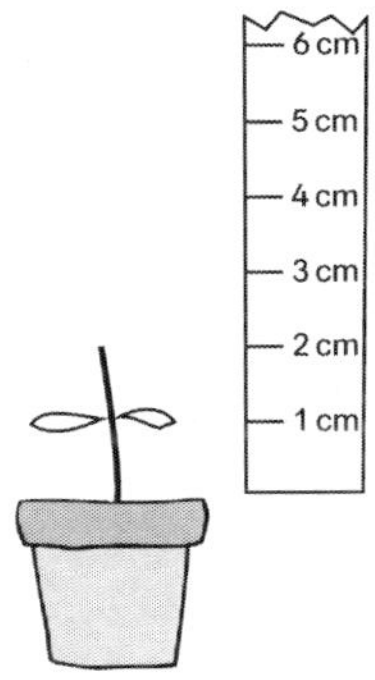

day 2

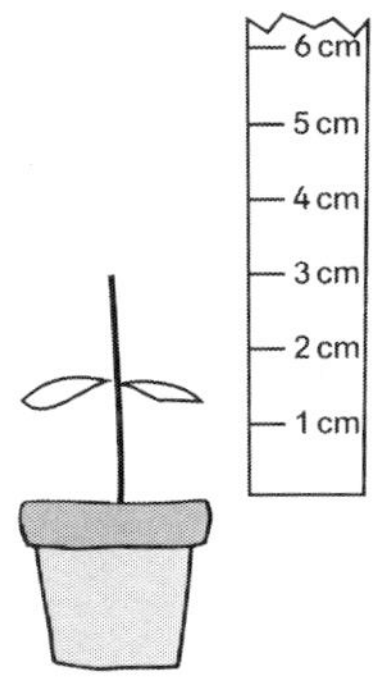

day 3

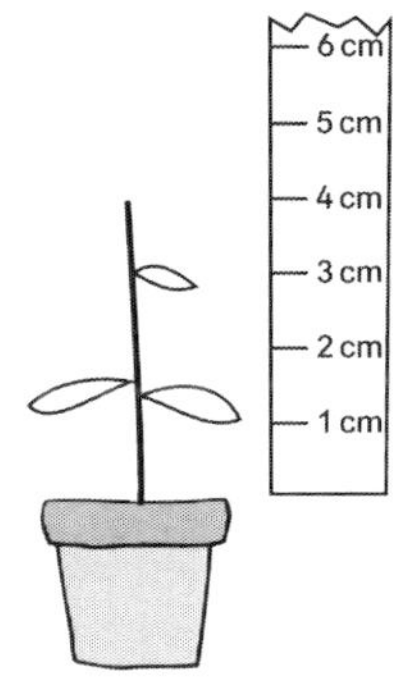

day 4

The plant grows.
Here is a bar chart showing how it has grown.

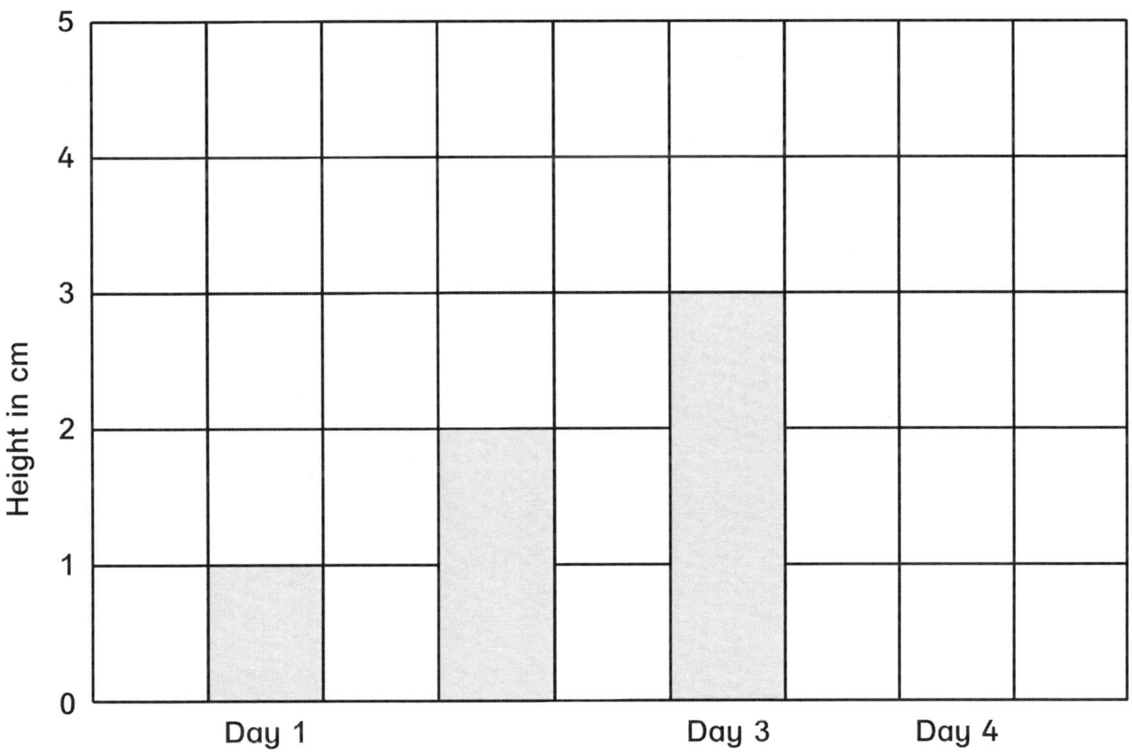

a) Fill in the label under the second bar.

b) Draw the bar for day 4.

A/WS
1 mark

A/WS
1 mark

Total for this page

5. **a)** Label the parts of the daffodil.

roots

flower

bulb

leaves

stem

KU

2 marks

b) Ajay planted these in the garden.

What will happen to them in the spring?

....

....

A

1 mark

/10

Total for this test

Year 1

Animals, including humans

Test 1 (diagnostic assessment)

Question	Answer	Extra information
1. A cat is an animal you can keep as a pet. Can you name a different animal that you can keep as a pet?	Specific name of any suitable animal	
2. A robin is a kind of bird. Can you name a different kind of bird?	Specific name of any kind of bird	
3. Can you name these animals?	Specific names of animals: whale, cat, pig	*Show the photographs provided on page 22.*
4. Can you name an animal that only eats meat?	Any carnivore, e.g. lion, tiger, shark, cat	Some cats are fed on things other than meat.
5. Name the main body parts of this animal.	Nose, tail, legs, ears	*Show the photograph provided on page 23.* Prompt by pointing to the parts if necessary.
6. What part of the body is this? What does it do?	Eyes to see, ears to hear, tongue to taste, fingers to feel, nose to smell	*Show the photograph provided on page 24.* Point to eyes, ears, tongue, fingers, nose.

Animals, including humans

Test 1 (diagnostic assessment): pupil responses form

Q	Some pupils	Most pupils	All pupils
1.			
2.			
3.			
4.			
5.			
6.			

Year 1

Animals, including humans

Test 1 (diagnostic assessment): question 3, visual prompts

Year 1

Animals, including humans

Test 1 (diagnostic assessment): question 5, visual prompts

Year 1

Animals, including humans

Test 1 (diagnostic assessment): question 6, visual prompt

Year 1

Animals, including humans Test 2 (mid-topic)

Name: ______________________ Class: ______________ Date: __________

1. Tick the animals.

man ☐

tree ☐

bird ☐

dandelion ☐

cow ☐

KU ☐ 2 marks

2. Write the name of each animal.

....

....

....

....

KU ☐ 2 marks

3. Here are two birds.
The swan is white. The hen is not white.
Write **one** other way they look different.

swan

hen

....

A/WS ☐ 1 mark

☐ Total for this page

4. **a)** Sort these animals into **two** groups. Draw arrows.

wasp

bear

dog

kangaroo

bird

have wings

no wings

A/WS

1 mark

A/WS

2 marks

b) Write the name of **one** more animal in each group.

5. **a)** All of these animals eat the same thing. What do they eat?

....

KU

1 mark

b) Do dogs eat the same thing? Circle the correct answer.

yes **no**

A

1 mark

/10

Total for this test

Year 1

Animals, including humans Test 3 (end of topic)

Name: __________________ Class: __________ Date: ________

1. Label the parts of the body.

foot

neck

knee

hand

KU

2 marks

2. **a)** Write **one** thing about the boy's body that is **different** from the dog's body.

....

A/WS

1 mark

b) Write **one** thing that the boy and the dog can both do.

....

A

1 mark

Total for this page

3. **a)** Label each part of the body and write its name in the box. Use the clues to help you.

You hear with this.

....

You see with this.

....

You taste with this.

....

You smell with this.

....

KU

2 marks

b) What part of your body would you use to touch something?

....

KU

1 mark

4. This graph shows the hair colour of the children in Class 1. Four children have brown hair.

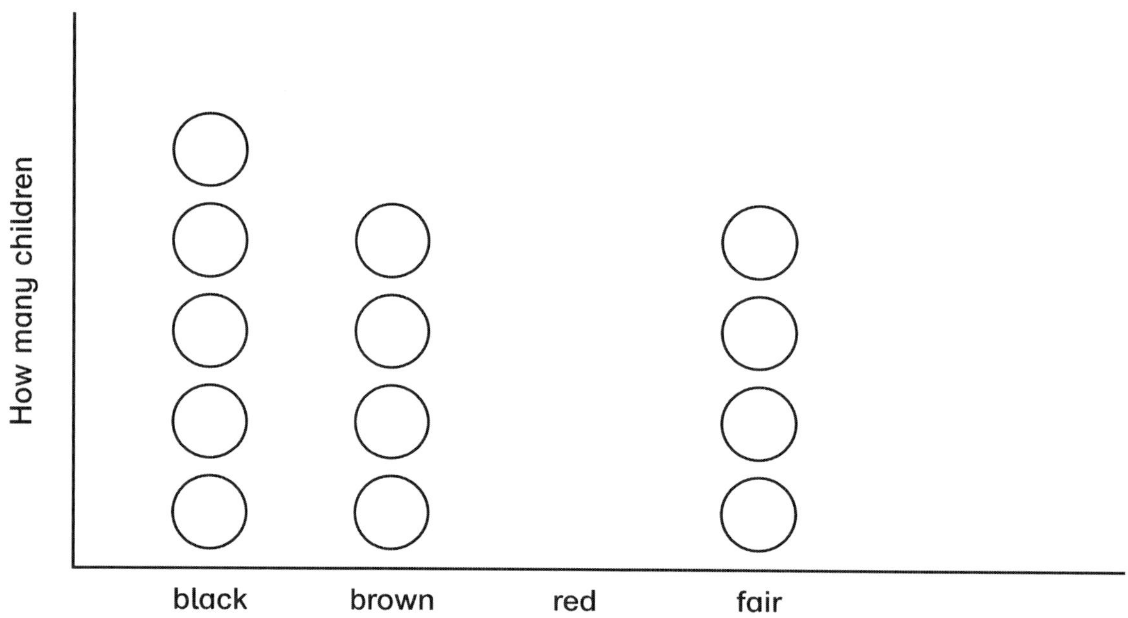

A/WS

1 mark

a) Two children have red hair. Draw them on the chart.

A/WS

1 mark

b) How many children have black hair? ....

A/WS

1 mark

c) Their teacher has grey hair. Add her to the graph.

/10

Total for this test

Year 1

Animals, including humans Test 4 (end of year)

Name: ____________________ Class: ____________ Date: __________

1. How many legs does each animal have? Fill in the table.

Animal	Legs	Animal	Legs
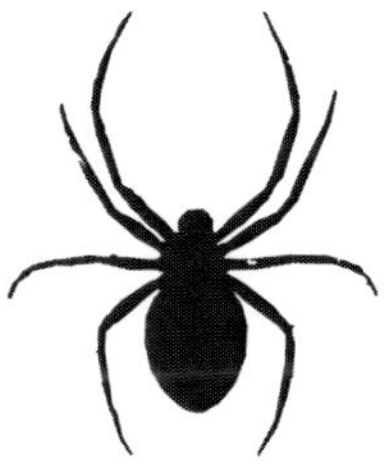			

A/WS

2 marks

2. Here is an arm. Label each part.

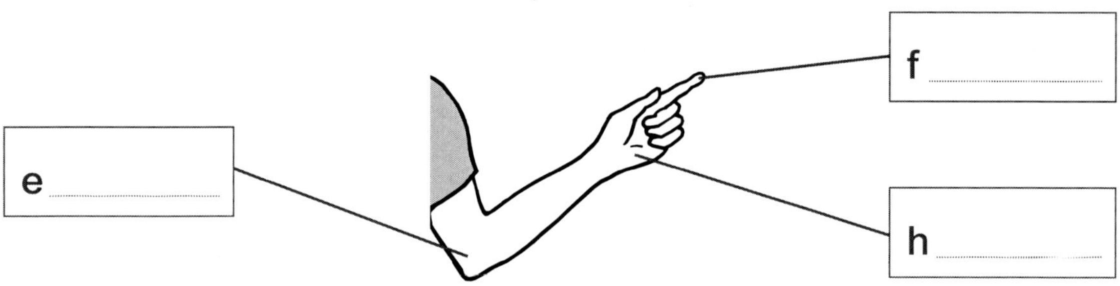

KU

2 marks

Total for this page

3. **a)** Ola is finding out about what animals eat.
She finds out that some animals only eat meat.
Tick the animal that eats only meat.

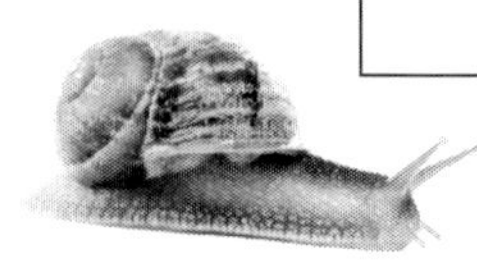

A/WS ☐ 1 mark

b) Write the name of an animal that eats only plants.
Write the name of one animal that is not in the pictures above.

....

KU ☐ 1 mark

c) How could Ola find out what elephants eat?

....

....

A/WS ☐ 1 mark

4. **a)** Label the parts of the fish.

KU ☐ 2 marks

b) Which part does the fish use to see with?

....

A ☐ 1 mark

/10 **Total for this test**

Year 1

Everyday materials Test 1 (diagnostic assessment)

Question	Answer	Extra information
1. Tell me the name of this object and say what it is made of.	Answer shows that children can distinguish between the object and what it is made from	*Use any suitable real object or show the picture of a pencil provided on page 32.* Some objects have the same name as the materials they are made from, e.g. a rock. Therefore, do not choose to show these objects.
2. Tell me what some things are made of.	Any common material, e.g. wood, plastic, metal	If it occurs, the term material may need explaining as 'what things are made of'. Note that the term 'material' is often used to mean 'fabric'.
3. Can you tell me what these objects are made of?	Any common material identified, e.g. glass, fabric/fleece, metal	*Use real materials or show the pictures of a window, a coat and a saucepan provided on page 33.*
4. Tell me something about this metal spoon. What does it look like? What does it feel like?	Any physical property identified, e.g. shiny, hard	*Use a real metal spoon or show the picture provided on page 34.* Children may need prompting to focus on the properties of metal rather than the shape and use of the object.
5. What is different about these two materials?	Any differences, e.g. metal is shiny; paper is bendy	Show two real objects made of two different materials, e.g. paper and metal, and allow the children to feel them.
6. Sort these materials by how they look or feel.	Objects sorted according to their properties, e.g. hard and soft; bendy and rigid	*Use real objects or show the pictures of a scarf, paper, a mug and a ruler provided on page 35.*

Everyday materials

Test 1 (diagnostic assessment): pupil responses form

Q	Some pupils	Most pupils	All pupils
1.			
2.			
3.			
4.			
5.			
6.			

Year 1

Everyday materials

Test 1 (diagnostic assessment): question 1, visual prompt

Year 1

Everyday materials

Test 1 (diagnostic assessment): question 3, visual prompts

Year 1

Everyday materials

Test 1 (diagnostic assessment): question 4, visual prompt

Year 1

Everyday materials

Test 1 (diagnostic assessment): question 6, visual prompts

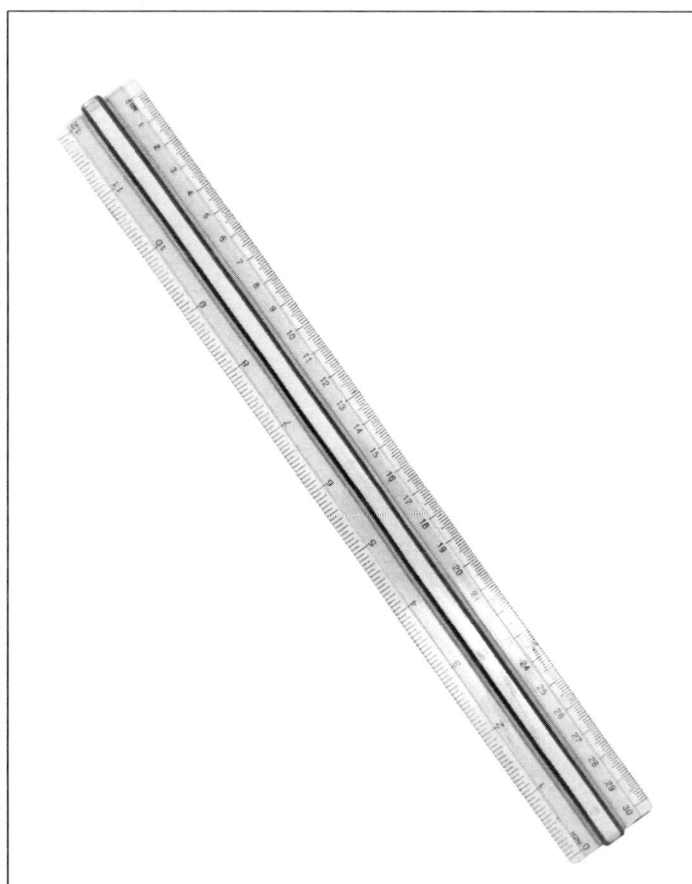

Year 1

Everyday materials Test 2 (mid-topic)

Name: ______________________ Class: ______________ Date: __________

1. Ella is looking at some things. She wants to see what they are made of. She sorts them into **two** groups.

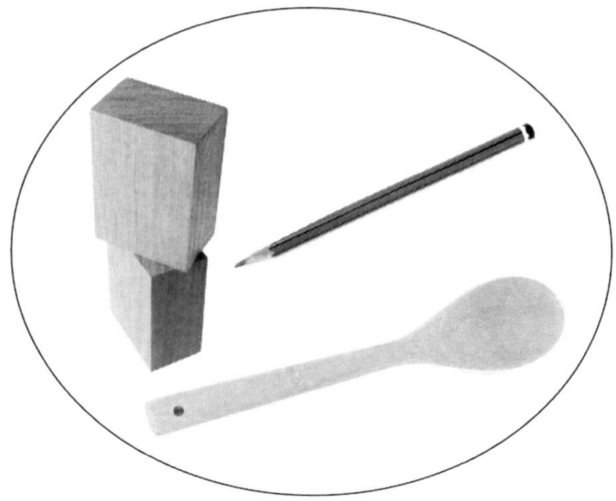

....

a) Write the name of what the things are made of under each group.

KU — 2 marks

b) Could Ella put her coat in one of the circles?
Circle the correct answer.

yes **no**

A — 1 mark

c) Why?

....

A/WS — 1 mark

d) Ella wants to find out if these things are hard or soft.
How can she find out?

....

A/WS — 1 mark

e) What does she find out?

....

A/WS — 1 mark

Total for this page

2. a) Tick the things but are made of metal.

paperclip

key

pin

marble

wool

teacup

needle

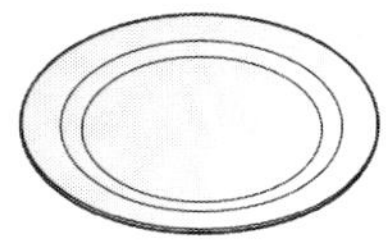
plate

KU
2 marks

b) Write the name of another thing made of metal.

....

KU
1 mark

3. Tick the things which are soft.

brick

plate

cat's fur

jumper

table

A/WS
1 mark

/10
Total for this test

Year 1

Everyday materials Test 3 (end of topic)

Name: ____________________ Class: __________ Date: __________

1. **a)** Draw lines to label the other things. Use each label once.

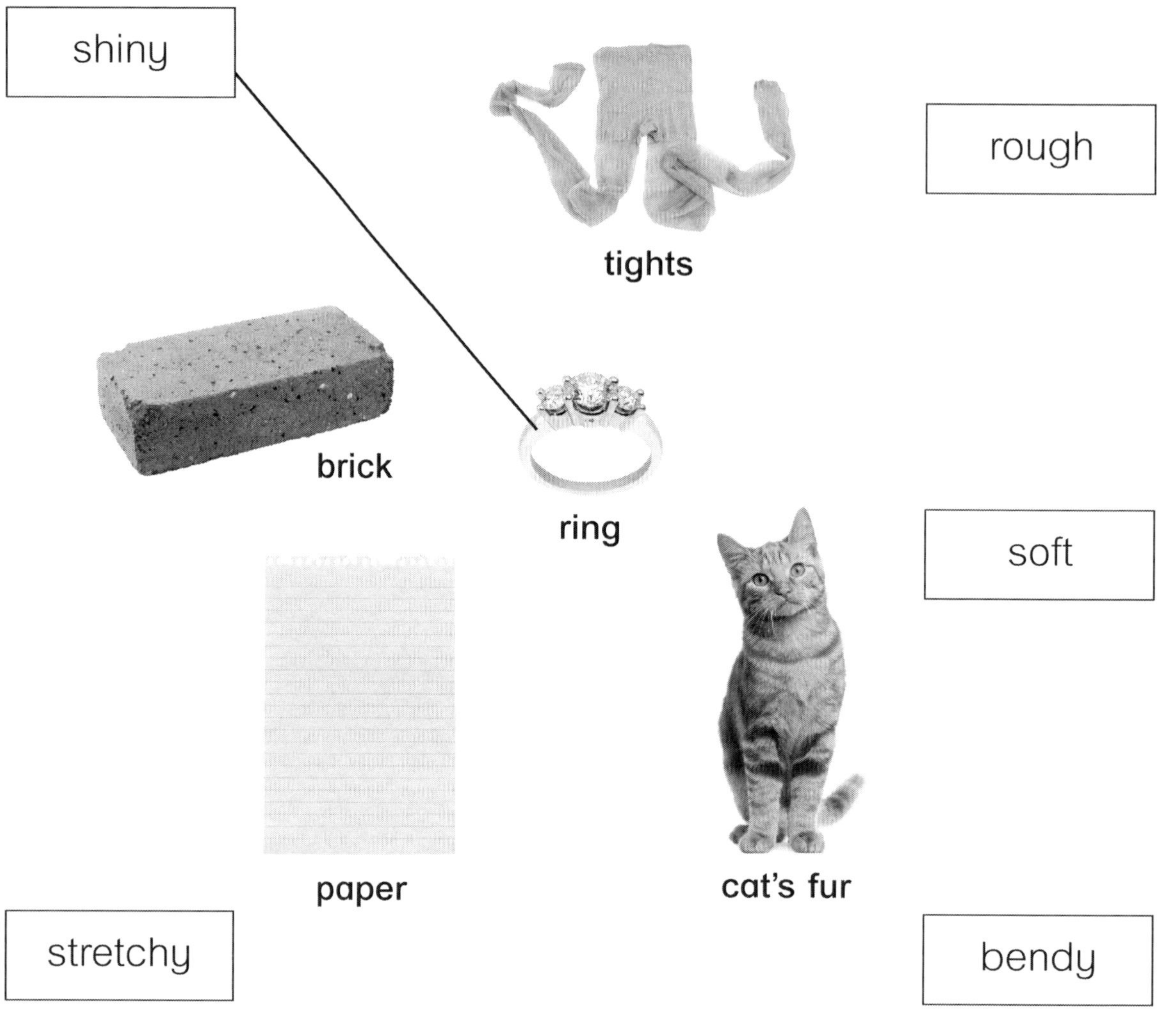

KU

2 marks

b) Write the name of **one** other thing that is shiny.

....

A

1 mark

Total for this page

2. These children felt some things hidden inside a bag.
They said:

a) Who do you think is wrong?

....

A/WS 1 mark

b) What could be **one** of the hard things in the bag?

....

KU 1 mark

c) What could be **two** of the soft things in the bag?

.... and ....

KU 2 marks

Total for this page

3. **a)** Milly has three bits of card.

plain card

cardboard

birthday card

She wants to find out if one card is different from the other two.
She does three tests.
Draw lines to show why she does each test.

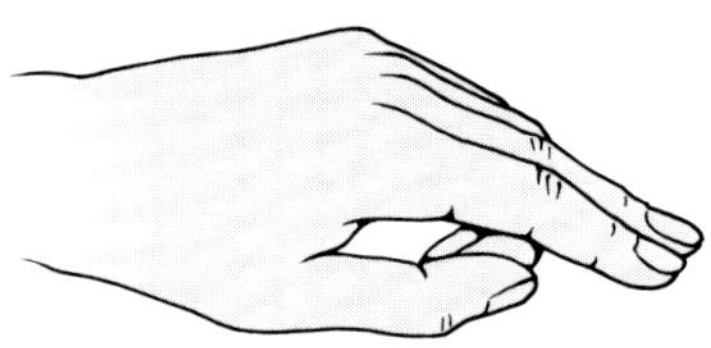

Feel them

To find out if they are rough or smooth

Look at them

To find out if they are bendy or stiff

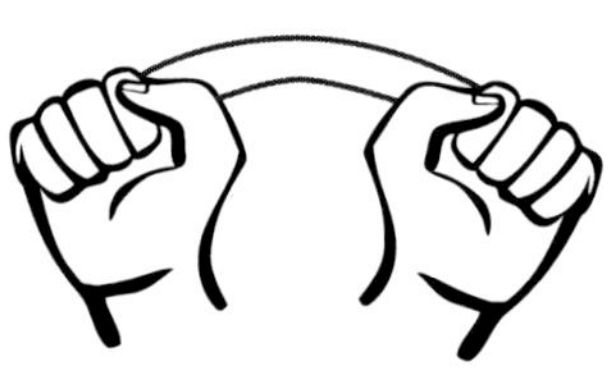

Bend them

To find out if they are shiny or dull

A/WS

2 marks

b) How could Milly find out if she can see through the cards?

....

A/WS

1 mark

/10

Total for this test

Year 1

Everyday materials Test 4 (end of year)

Name: ______________________ Class: ______________ Date: __________

1. a) Sort these materials into two groups. Draw arrows.

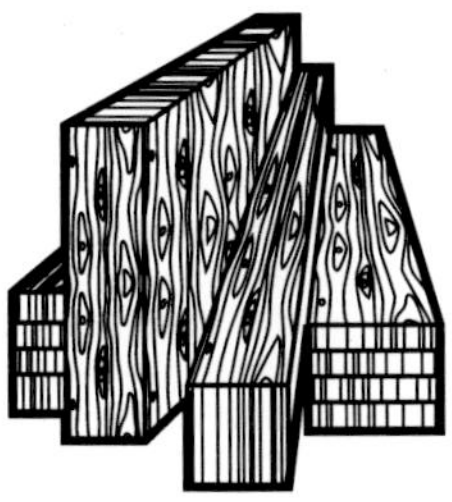

wood

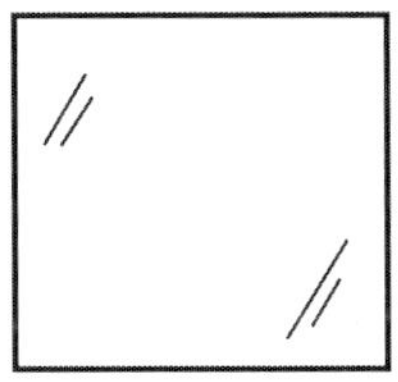

glass

stone

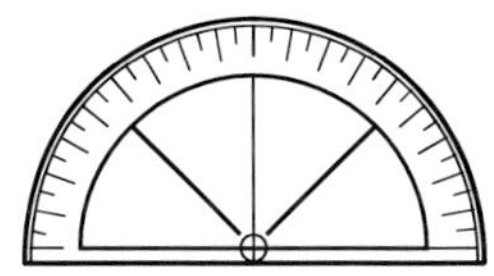

plastic

plain card

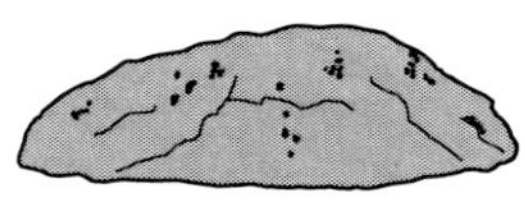

sand

see through

not see through

KU

2 marks

b) Write the name of **one** other thing you could put in the 'not see through' group.

....

A

1 mark

Total for this page

2. Here are two cups.

china cup

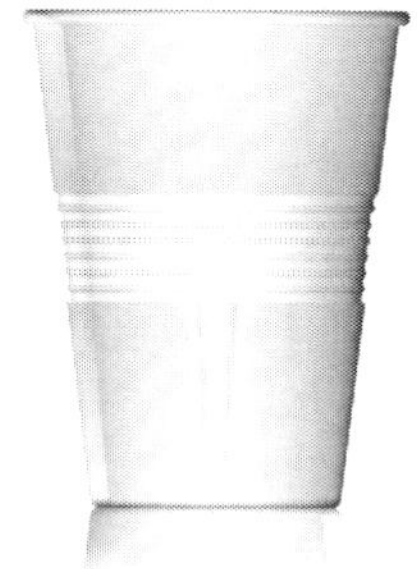

plastic cup

a) Why is china a good material to make a cup from?

....

KU

1 mark

b) Why is plastic a good material to make a cup from?

....

KU

1 mark

c) Write down one way the plastic cup is different to the china cup.

....

KU

1 mark

3. **a)** Li wants to find a good material to make an umbrella.
She drips water onto some materials.
She watches to see which materials let the water through.
Fill in the gaps in the table.

Material	**Water went through**
plastic	
tissue	
paper	✓
towel	

A/WS

2 marks

b) What should Li make her umbrella out of? ....

Why? ....

....

A/WS

2 marks

/10

Total for this test

Year 1

Seasonal changes Test 1 (diagnostic assessment)

Question		Answer	Extra information
1.	Can you tell me the names of the four seasons?	Spring, summer, autumn, winter	
2.	What season do you think this is?	Relates clothing and place to the season	*Use the photographs provided on pages 44–45.*
3.	Can you tell me some of the differences between autumn and winter?	Any seasonal changes relating to weather or day length	Accept any answer that refers to plant growth or animal behaviour
4.	What is the weather like in summer?	Any answer regarding temperature, rainfall or sunshine typically related to summer, e.g. it is hot and sunny	
5.	Can you tell me the difference between when it is dark in summer and winter?	The days are longer in summer than in winter.	Accept any answer which demonstrates an awareness of the difference in when it gets light in the morning or dark in the evening in either summer or winter

Seasonal changes

Test 1 (diagnostic assessment): pupil responses form

Q	Some pupils	Most pupils	All pupils
1.			
2.			
3.			
4.			
5.			

Year 1

Seasonal changes

Test 1 (diagnostic assessment): question 2, visual prompts

Year 1

Seasonal changes

Test 1 (diagnostic assessment): question 2, visual prompts

Year 1
Seasonal changes Test 2 (mid-topic)

Name: ______________________ Class: ______________ Date: __________

1.

summer	spring	winter	autumn

a) Match the picture to the season.
Draw a line to the correct word.

KU
1 mark

b) Put the seasons in order. Put numbers in the box in the corner of each picture.

KU
1 mark

c) Which is the hottest season? ....

KU
1 mark

d) Which is the coldest season? ....

KU
1 mark

Total for this page

2. Why doesn't it snow in the summer?

....

A
1 mark

3. **a)** Class 1 made a record of the weather for one week.

Day	**Weather**
Monday	
Tuesday	
Wednesday	
Thursday	
Friday	

On Wednesday it was raining.
On Friday it was sunny.
Fill in the table.

A/WS
2 marks

b) Which day was cloudy? ....

A/WS
1 mark

c) On which days did the children need to wear sun hats at playtime?

.... and ....

A/WS
1 mark

d) Why is it important to wear a sun hat?

....

....

KU
1 mark

/10
Total for this test

Year 1

Seasonal changes Test 3 (end of topic)

Name: ______________________ Class: ______________ Date: __________

1. **a)** Class 1 wanted to find out how cold it was each day.
What did they use to measure the temperature?
Tick the correct answer.

☐

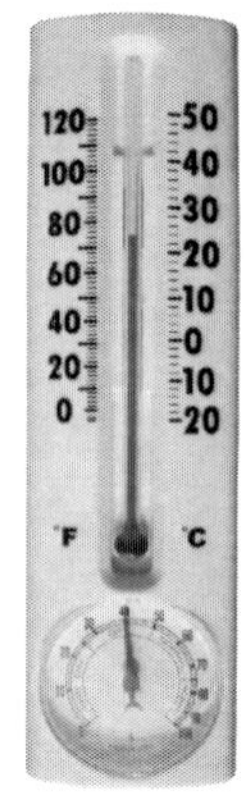

☐

☐

☐

A/WS
1 mark

b) Where did they put it? ....

A
1 mark

c) Which shows the coldest temperature?
Tick the correct answer.

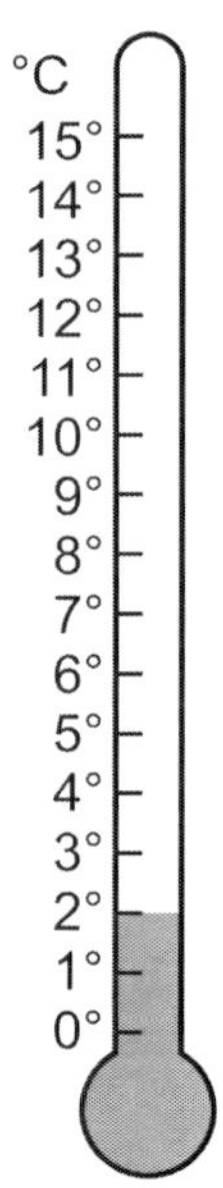

☐

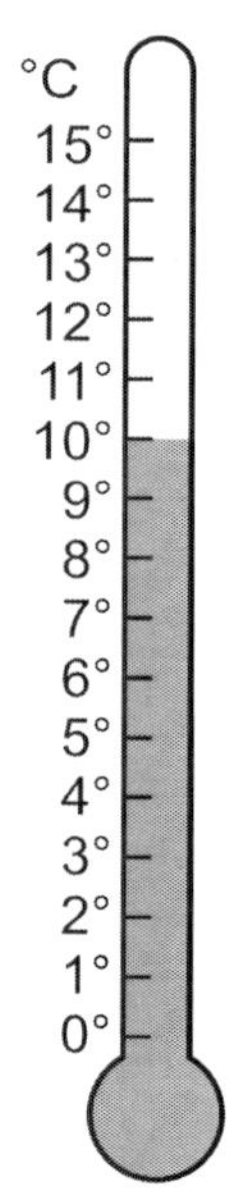

☐

A/WS
1 mark

Total for this page

1. d) The children recorded the temperature in their playground on a bar chart.

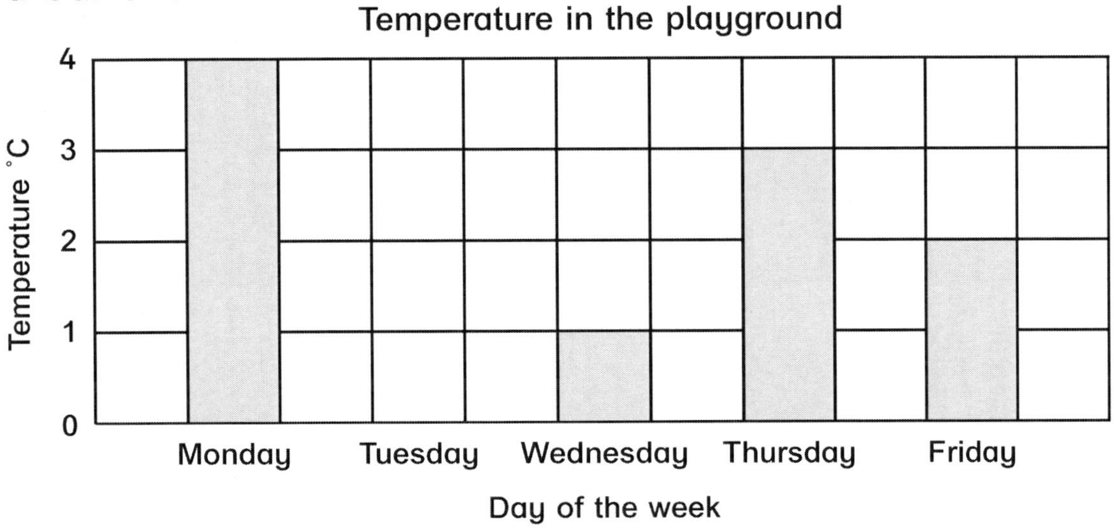

On Tuesday it was 2°C.

Draw the bar on the chart.

A/WS ☐ 1 mark

e) Which season do you think it was? ....

KU ☐ 1 mark

f) How do you know? ....

....

A/WS ☐ 1 mark

2. Tick summer or winter for each child to show what season it is.

a. It is light when I go to bed.

summer ☐ winter ☐

b. It is dark when I get up in the morning.

summer ☐ winter ☐

c. It is dark when I go to bed.

summer ☐ winter ☐

d. It is light when I get up in the morning.

summer ☐ winter ☐

KU ☐ 2 marks

☐ Total for this page

3. Circle the correct answer.

a) In summer the days are than in winter. **longer** **shorter**

KU

1 mark

b) In winter the days are than in summer. **longer** **shorter**

KU

1 mark

/10

Total for this test

Year 1

Seasonal changes Test 4 (end of year)

Name: ______________________ Class: ______________ Date: __________

1. There is a tree in the playground.
Class 1 drew the tree during the year.
Join each picture to the correct season.

summer	autumn	spring	winter

KU
2 marks

2. Class 1 planted some daffodil bulbs in the school garden just before the Christmas holidays.

a) After Christmas, the bulbs had not grown. Why?

....

....

A
1 mark

b) When did they start to grow?

....

KU
1 mark

Total for this page

3. The sun is shining. Complete the sentences below.

The boy must not look at the ....

It can ....

KU

2 marks

4. **a)** Class 1 made a record of the weather for one week.

Day	**Weather**	**Temperature °C**
Monday	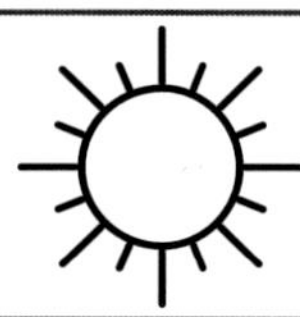	20
Tuesday		14
Wednesday		
Thursday		
Friday		18

Put these temperatures where you think they should go in the table.

21 13

A/WS

2 marks

b) Which was the hottest day? ....

A/WS

1 mark

c) What did the children use to measure the temperature?

....

A/WS

1 mark

/10

Total for this test

Answers and mark schemes

Year 1 Plants*

* Accept phonically plausible spellings for all answers.

Test 2 (mid-topic)	Area	Mark	Extra information
1. Labels joined correctly 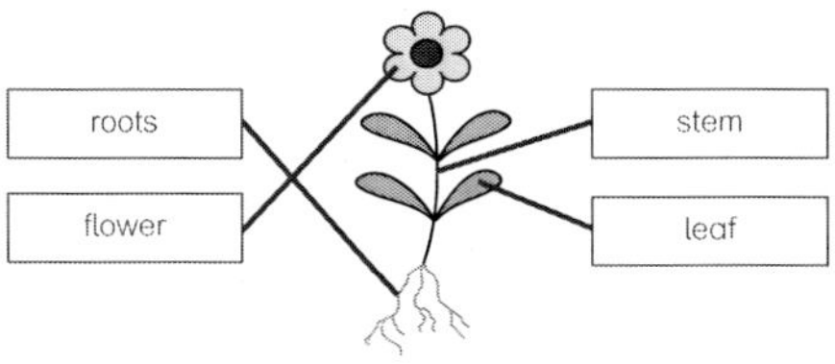	KU	2	2 marks for all four correct 1 mark for two or three correct
2a. Any **two** differences that refer to shape, size or number of petals	KU	2	1 mark for each correct. Accept an answer which does not name the petal as long as the meaning is clear
2b. Petal	KU	1	
3a. Magnifying glass ticked	A/WS	1	
3b. Look through it or hold it to your eye.	A	1	
4a. Suitable grouping based on features of leaves, e.g. elm, lime, beech in one group and sycamore and maple in the other (based on similar shapes).	A/WS	1	
4b. An explanation of grouping based on features.	A/WS	1	
4c. Accept a drawing in either group that shows a leaf with similar features (e.g. shape if that was the grouping used in 4a).	A/WS	1	

Plants (continued)

<table>
<tr><th>Test 3 (end of topic)</th><th>Area</th><th>Mark</th><th>Extra information</th></tr>
<tr><td>1a. Labels joined correctly
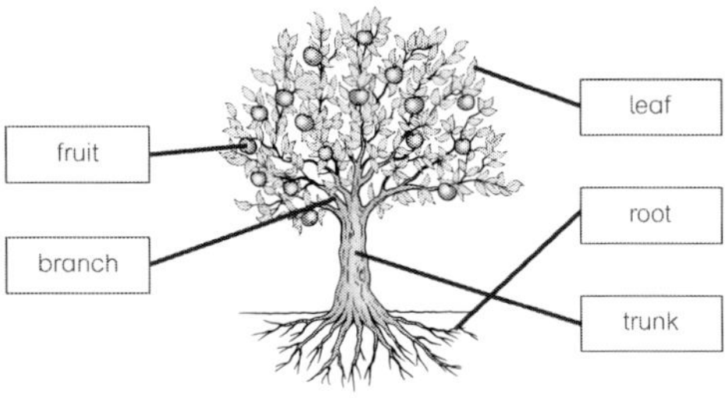
</td><td>KU</td><td>2</td><td>2 marks for all five correct
1 mark for two to four correct</td></tr>
<tr><td>1b. It is winter/autumn.
The tree has died.</td><td>KU</td><td>1</td><td>Accept any suitable reference to change in season
Accept it is deciduous or it has not had enough water</td></tr>
<tr><td>1c. They turn brown/change colour.
They die.</td><td>KU</td><td>1</td><td>Accept any answer which indicates a physical change</td></tr>
<tr><td>2. Name of any specific tree.</td><td>KU</td><td>1</td><td>Accept any specific fruit tree (e.g. apple)
Accept pine/Christmas tree</td></tr>
<tr><td>3a. Shows two leaves.
Shows five roots.</td><td>A/WS</td><td>1
1</td><td></td></tr>
<tr><td>3b.
<table>
<tr><th>Day</th><th>Number of leaves</th><th>Number of roots</th></tr>
<tr><td>1</td><td>2</td><td>2</td></tr>
<tr><td>2</td><td>2</td><td>3</td></tr>
<tr><td>3</td><td>2</td><td>5</td></tr>
<tr><td>4</td><td>3</td><td>6</td></tr>
</table></td><td>A/WS</td><td>2</td><td>1 mark for day 2 correct
1 mark for day 4 correct</td></tr>
<tr><td>3c. It has grown. It is longer.</td><td>A</td><td>1</td><td>Accept any reference to the stem being longer than day 2 or shorter than day 4</td></tr>
</table>

Test 4 (end of year)	Area	Mark	Extra information
1. It will look the same.	KU	1	Accept any answer referring to the tree being an evergreen tree or not losing its leaves
2a. Trees	KU	1	
2b. Any **one** from: dandelion is light or small or has a parachute Any **one** from: acorn is hard or big or round	A/WS	1 1	Answer needs to imply a comparison Accept that the acorn is in a cup
3. Cauliflower and pea ticked	KU	1	Both ticked for 1 mark
4a. 'Day 2' written under bar.	A/WS	1	
4b. Bar drawn to height of 4 cm.	A/WS	1	Minimal tolerance of height; ignore width
5a. Labels all joined correctly	KU	2	2 marks for all 5 correct 1 mark for two to four correct
5b. They started to grow.	A	1	Accept any indication of growth, e.g. leaves appear, they have shoots or flowers

Animals, including humans

Test 2 (mid-topic)	Area	Mark	Extra information
1. Man, cow, bird ticked	KU	2	2 marks for all three correct 1 mark for two correct
2. Correct names written alongside each animal. 	KU	2	2 marks for all four correct 1 mark for two or three correct Accept pony instead of horse
3. Any **one** from: size, length of neck, beak size	A/WS	1	Accept that the swan is swimming
4a. Have wings: wasp, bird No wings: bear, dog, kangaroo	A/WS	1	
4b. A suitable animal and its name added to each group.	A/WS	2	1 mark for each animal
5a. Grass	KU	1	Accept plants
5b. No	A	1	Note: dogs occasionally eat grass for medicinal reasons

Test 3 (end of topic)	Area	Mark	Extra information
1. Parts of body correctly labelled 	KU	2	2 marks for all four correct 1 mark for two or three correct
2a. Any **one** physical feature that is **different**, e.g. shape of face, number of legs, tail	A/WS	1	
2b. Any **one** activity they can both do, e.g. run, see, hear	A	1	
3a. All labels joined to correct features 	KU	1 1	1 mark for all features correctly identified by labels 1 mark for names of all features in boxes
3b. Hand or fingers	KU	1	Accept skin, nose, cheek, toe, foot or any other appropriate part of the body
4a. Two circles added to red column.	A/WS	1	
4b. 5	A/WS	1	
4c. 'Grey' added on the line and one shape added.	A/WS	1	

Animals, including humans (continued)

Test 4 (end of year)	Area	Mark	Extra information
1. Spider 8, gorilla 2, deer 4, fly 6	A/WS	2	2 marks for all four correct 1 mark for two or three correct
2. Elbow, hand, finger	KU	2	2 marks for all three correct 1 mark for two correct
3a. Lion ticked	A/WS	1	
3b. Any herbivore, e.g. horse, goat, rabbit	KU	1	Do not accept cow or snail
3c. Look it up in a book Look it up on a computer Watch one in a zoo.	A/WS	1	Accept any feasible answer which would give the correct information, including asking someone
4a. Parts correctly labelled 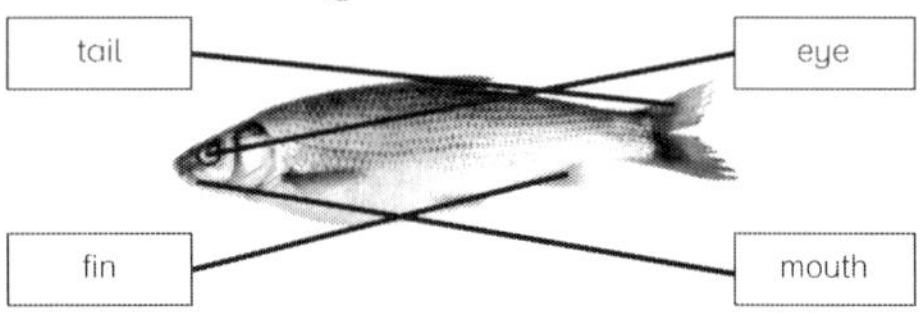	KU	2	2 marks for all four correct 1 mark for two or three correct
4b. Eye	A	1	

Everyday materials

Test 2 (mid-topic)	Area	Mark	Extra information
1a. Plastic, wood	KU	2	1 mark for each correct
1b. No	A	1	
1c. It is not made of wood or plastic. It is made of fabric or fleece or wool.	A/WS	1	Accept if answer only states it is not made of either wood or plastic or that a coat is made of something else
1d. Feel them.	A/WS	1	Accept any other feasible way of testing the objects, e.g. touch them, bite them
1e. They are all hard.	A/WS	1	
2a. Key, paperclip, pin, needle ticked	KU	2	2 marks for all four correct 1 mark for two or three correct
2b. Any object made from metal	KU	1	Accept anything which is made of more than one material including metal
3. Jumper and cat's fur	A/WS	1	1 mark for both correct

Test 3 (end of topic)	Area	Mark	Extra information
1a. Tights: stretchy; brick: rough; cat's fur: soft; paper: bendy	KU	2	2 marks for all four correct 1 mark for two or three correct
1b. Any object which reflects light, e.g. mirror, star, jewellery	A	1	
2a. Ryan	A/WS	1	
2b. Any **one** hard material or object, e.g. stone, coin, pen, book, box	KU	1	
2c. Any **two** soft materials or objects, e.g. fur, wool, sock, doll	KU	2	1 mark for each correct
3a. Labels correctly joined Feel them – to find out if they are rough or smooth Look at them – to find out if they are shiny or dull Bend them – to find out if they are bendy or stiff	A/WS	2	2 marks for three correct 1 mark for one correct
3b. Hold them up to the light or window. Look through them.	A/WS	1	Accept hold them up to her eyes or try to read through them

Everyday materials (continued)

Test 4 (end of year)	Area	Mark	Extra information
1a. See through – glass, plastic Not see through – wood, sand, stone, plain card	KU	2	2 marks for all six correct 1 mark for three to five correct
1b. Any opaque material or object	A	1	
2a. It is hard or strong or waterproof. It does not let the drink go through. It does not break easily.	KU	1	Accept reference to any physical property that makes china suitable for a cup
2b. It is hard or waterproof. It does not let the drink go through.	KU	1	Accept that the plastic cup is cheap or disposable or see through so that you can see what you are drinking
2c. It is see through. You can squash it; it breaks easily. It is light.	KU	1	Accept reference to any other physical property or that it is cheap or disposable
3a. plastic ✗, tissue ✓, towel ✓	A/WS	2	2 marks for three correct 1 mark for two correct
3b. Plastic Because it is waterproof.	A/WS A/WS	1 1	 Accept it will not let the water through

Seasonal changes

Test 2 (mid-topic)	Area	Mark	Extra information
1a. Summer: sun; autumn: wind; winter: snow	KU	1	1 mark for all correct
1b. 2 summer, 3 autumn, 4 winter	KU	1	1 mark for all correct
1c. Summer	KU	1	
1d. Winter	KU	1	
2. It is too hot	A	1	Any indication of temperature not being suitable
3a. Rain symbol drawn in table for Wednesday. Sun symbol drawn in table for Friday.	A/WS	1 1	1 mark for each correct symbol
3b. Thursday	A/WS	1	
3c. Monday and Friday	A/WS	1	Both correct for 1 mark Accept additional inclusion of Thursday
3d. So the sun does not burn you. To keep the sun out of your eyes. To protect you from the sun.	KU	1	Accept any reasonable answer for 1 mark and accept so you do not get ill

Test 3 (end of topic)	Area	Mark	Extra information
1a. Thermometer ticked	A/WS	1	
1b. Outside or in the playground	A	1	Accept any answer referring to the thermometer being outside
1c. Thermometer showing 2°C ticked	A/WS	1	
1d. Bar drawn to height of 2°	A/WS	1	Accept any width of bar
1e. Winter	KU	1	
1f. It is cold or the temperature is low.	A/WS	1	Accept any answer which indicates that it is cold
2. Child a: summer; child b: winter; child c: winter; child d: summer	KU	2	2 marks for all correct 1 mark for two or three correct
3a. Longer	KU	1	
3b. Shorter	KU	1	

Seasonal changes (continued)

Test 4 (end of year)	Area	Mark	Extra information
1. Summer: tree in full leaf Autumn: tree with leaves falling Winter: tree with no leaves	KU	2	2 marks for all correct 1 mark for one correct
2a. Because it was winter. Because it was (too) cold.	A	1	
2b. In the spring. When it got warmer.	KU	1	
3. Sun hurt your eyes.	KU	1 1	 Accept any reference to damaging eyesight or it is too bright or strong
4a. Wednesday 21 Thursday 13	A/WS	1 1	
4b. Wednesday	A/WS	1	
4c. Thermometer	A/WS	1	